*Great stables for the great house. These at Chatsworth, Derbyshire, were designed by James Paine, 1756.*

# STABLES AND STABLE BLOCKS

Christopher Powell

Shire Publications Ltd

CONTENTS



 *First published 1991. Shire Album 261. ISBN 0 7478 0105 3.*


Printed in Great Britain by C. I. Thomas & Sons (Haverfordwest) Ltd, Press Buildings, Merlins Bridge, Haverfordwest, Dyfed SA61 1XF.

British Library Cataloguing in Publication Data: Powell, Christopher, 1941-. Stables and stable blocks. 1. Stables. Outdoor manèges. Construction & maintenance. I. Title. 636. 1083. ISBN 0-7478-0105-3.

ACKNOWLEDGEMENTS
The author is grateful to the following for their assistance: J. Anson; M. Bone; the proprietors of Breamore House; Bristol City Council; Cogges Farm Museum; R. Grynyer; Gordon Kelsey; D. J. Leighton; B. J. Powell; Shugborough Estate. The cover and the illustrations on pages 1, 13 (bottom), 15 (bottom left), 18 and 32 are acknowledged to Cadbury Lamb.

Cover: *Stables for the country house: Moccas Court, Herefordshire.*

Below: *Stables for the ironworks of Sir John Guest at Dowlais, Mid Glamorgan, 1820.*

*The Archbishop's Stables, Maidstone, Kent. This fourteenth-century building was subsequently used by a tanner before becoming the Tyrwhitt-Drake Museum of Carriages.*

# ORIGINS

The stables of England and Wales are a remarkable building type: attractive, varied, once common in town and country, yet not widely appreciated. This book introduces their great range by looking at three groups, based on ownership. They are farm stables, stables with houses, and stables for businesses and institutions. The first group was built mainly by local craftsmen in local styles. Most stables with houses were designed more consciously, and the third group, for businesses, was often plain and functional. Some stables, though seen by many people, are not recognised for what they are, and others are not even noticed. All deserve to be more appreciated.

This book puts the fabric of stables into historical context and looks at their form and materials. This approach helps to show how social and economic influences gave rise to particular kinds of buildings in particular places and times.

The origins of stables in Britain are obscure. Roman remains have been found, but they are only of small buildings which survive fragmentarily. Little survives from the Saxon period, but there are some buildings and documentary evidence from medieval times. For example, there is record of Edward I's hunting-lodge stable of 1282 at Clipstone, near Mansfield, Nottinghamshire. Fragments are found in castles and monasteries. At Canterbury, Kent, a gateway block in Green Court is said to have belonged to a stable yard. A fourteenth-century record survives of royal stables at Sheen, Surrey, which were 32 metres long and 9.1 metres high (105 by 30 feet). Again, there is an undertaking of 1342 by a carpenter, William of Fulbourne, to build two oak-framed stables complete with all masonry, ironwork, plasterwork and tiling, for £80. Bolton Castle, North Yorkshire, after 1375 had stables beneath guests' rooms and at Goodrich Castle, Herefordshire, stables were added in the fourteenth century. About the same time a stable block was built in Maidstone, Kent, for the Archbishop of Canterbury and it still survives. Another early survivor is the ruined late sixteenth-century block added at Ludlow Castle, Shropshire.

Early examples like these serving royal,

church and military needs are often very incomplete or much altered and hence difficult to understand today. The stables built later for those owners were increasingly overshadowed in size and number by stables for the houses of the rising classes of noblemen and merchants. The age of grand stables for the houses of important individuals was dawning, but before this story is taken further another thread of development is taken up.

Left: *The remains of the late sixteenth-century stable block in the outer court at Ludlow Castle, Shropshire.*

Below: *Midland vernacular: a late eighteenth-century three-horse (perhaps originally oxen) farm stable from Wychbold, Worcestershire, now at Avoncroft Museum of Buildings, Bromsgrove, Worcestershire. It is of timber-frame construction infilled with brick, on a stone plinth. The gable is timber-clad and there are plain clay roof tiles.*

*This stable in the West Sussex vernacular style of timber frame and cladding with plain tile roof was built for a farm at Watersfield, probably in the eighteenth century. It is now at the Weald and Downland Open Air Museum, Singleton, West Sussex.*

# FARM STABLES

The era of heavy draught horses was a long one, lasting from the lingering decline of oxen, far gone by the late eighteenth century, to the rise of tractors during the Second World War. Horses were essential on almost every lowland holding of any size, for cultivation and haulage. On arable land there was work for one horse for about every 20-25 acres (8-10 ha); heavy soil demanded more horses than light land. The number used solely for agriculture reached a peak of about 900,000 shortly before the First World War, and its decline was not rapid, for as late as 1939 there were said to be eleven horses for every tractor. The importance of horse power to the farm conferred high status on these animals. No other farm animal was given so much care or looked on with such affection and pride. This was reflected in the form of stables, which compared well with cowsheds. Their importance was seen in building costs, which, in 1913, ranged from 6d to 10d per cubic foot, compared with only 4d to 6½d for workmen's cottages.

Many of the oldest surviving farm stables were arranged so that horses were tied in a position parallel to the line of the roof ridge. In this way three or four horses could be sheltered side by side, within the limits of simple roof spans. If more space was needed, a further three or four horses could be placed in a bigger stable tail to tail across a gangway from the first group. This type of stable could readily be attached to other farm buildings, sharing a gable wall. The type is found in small numbers from before the eighteenth century, and in larger numbers after. By that time British farming was becoming more and more progressive and much thought and experiment were given to improved methods and buildings.

Above: *Inside a farm stable at Rangeworthy, Avon. Left are a ladder, loft hatch, door and window. There are wooden harness hooks and a small cupboard recess in the plastered walls. The pitched stone floor slopes gently to a drainage channel. On the right are a wooden stall, a rack and a trough with a tethering ring. The last occupants were 'Prince' and 'Dolly' in the early 1950s. This stable had a working life of just over one hundred years.*

A more flexible arrangement of horses was with the stalls at right angles to the line of the roof ridge. This across-building layout allowed the number of horses to be varied, free from concern with roof span. This layout emerged early on but was not very widely used before the beginning of the nineteenth century. After that time the across-building layout gradually replaced the other pattern. The change probably took place first in advanced lowland regions, spreading later to the more remote uplands. The across-building layout had advantages of flexibility and more even ventilation and daylight. Appreciation of the importance of this to the well-being of horses gradually spread. Horses kept for lighter work, which might have less exercise, as well as foals and sick horses, were often housed in loose-boxes. These were spaces larger than stalls, in which the horse was kept untied. Some loose-boxes were partitioned off from the main area of stalls and others were separate rooms.

Most stables built before the later eighteenth century and many built after then had lofts over them. They provided heat insulation for the horses, which are susceptible to cold, and could be used for storing hay or straw. This was conveniently dropped through holes in the loft floor when required. Occasionally loft space was used as a granary or as sleeping space for farm labourers, a practice which lasted well into the twentieth century. Access to the loft was either by external masonry steps, often against a gable wall, or by ladder.

Stable exteriors often suggested buildings of better quality than any of the other farm buildings except the farmhouse. This was more likely in stables for riding and carriage horses than in those solely for heavy draught animals, and it applied to later buildings rather than earlier ones. Generous floor-to-ceiling heights (for better ventilation) of 2.5 to 2.75 metres (8-9 feet) added

Below: *Traditional materials: thatched roof, flint and brick walls (though the window frames have been replaced). The timber-clad great barn, right, and the timber-framed brick and tile granary, left, add harmonious variety to this group at Hurstbourne Tarrant, Hampshire.*

*Stables (centre) in their context. This pleasing farm group, with rubble walls and pantile roof, is at West Tanfield, North Yorkshire.*

dignity. Windows were usually larger than those of other farm buildings. Doorways were necessarily quite wide and fitted with horizontally split, two-flap doors. The range of building materials was wide and followed the gradual evolution of vernacular building methods. Before the earlier nineteenth century most materials were those readily found in the locality, avoiding the need for costly transport, and so the walls were of limestone in the Cotswolds, flint in parts of Norfolk, and so on. Many early roofs were thatched, but these were increasingly likely to be replaced on new and existing buildings with stone, slate or clay tiles (depending on region) as time went on. Many window and door openings were spanned in the simplest way with rough timber lintels. In the course of the nineteenth century easier transport allowed

*A Georgian farm stable, c.1770, at Acton Scott Working Farm Museum, Church Stretton, Shropshire. The stone plinth and gable ornament lend distinction to a simple brick box. The taller building on the left was built for carriage horses.*

Left: *Materials in detail: slate roof, rubble wall (here rather crudely re-pointed), brick arches, small-paned window, heavy hinges, attractively patterned and textured stone paving. This stable is at Tredegar House, Newport, Gwent.*

Right: *Farmyard simplicity: the exterior of the stable at Rangeworthy, Avon, shown in the diagram on page 6. It was built c.1840, next to a barn, left. Note the customary horseshoes hanging over the door.*

materials to be brought from a distance, so that distinctive local character and craftsmanship declined. Rough-hewn, semi-natural appearances gave way to more artificial materials. Many late nineteenth-century stables were built of hard brick with thin regular slate or clay tile roofs. Strident reds and blues as well as more muted colours were used, often brought many miles from large manufacturers. By that time, too,

*Later construction. This North Yorkshire example shows typical, heavily processed materials: thin slate roof, hard-brick walls, stout joinery, heavy window sills and triangular roof vent (just visible left of the tree).*

*Model stables at Shugborough Park Farm, Staffordshire, designed by Samuel Wyatt, 1805.*

shallow brick arches over windows and doors were being installed instead of perishable timber lintels.

External decoration was limited mainly to stables on better-off, larger farms. There, architectural aspirations might be towards the grandeur of large country-house stables. Decorations included circular pitching holes for loading the lofts, and cornerstones and the heads of windows and doors in brick or stone of contrasting colour. Sometimes there were curved Dutch gables, carved datestones and decorative ridge tiles. Most stables were plain and simple, hard-wearing workaday structures, attractive in a forthright way. Variety came from the materials, the proportions and the position of doors, windows and steps.

Some stables had a separate harness room opening off the stable. A few stables had a separate room for storage of feed. Individual stalls were usually provided, though sometimes horses were tethered in pairs, or without separation. Partitions between stalls were generally wooden, highest at the head (to restrict visibility), stout enough to resist leaning horses, and strong enough at the tail to withstand kicking. They were spaced about 1.5 to 1.8 metres (5-6 feet) apart. Paving sloped gently to a channel behind the horse. Cupboards, recessed into the wall or attached to it out of harm's way, held combs and medicine. There were large wall

Below: *Model interior. A tapering timber stall division and paved floor at Shugborough Park Farm. There is a high-level vent hole (upper left) in the whitewashed brick wall. Timber floor joists are visible above the rack, upper right.*

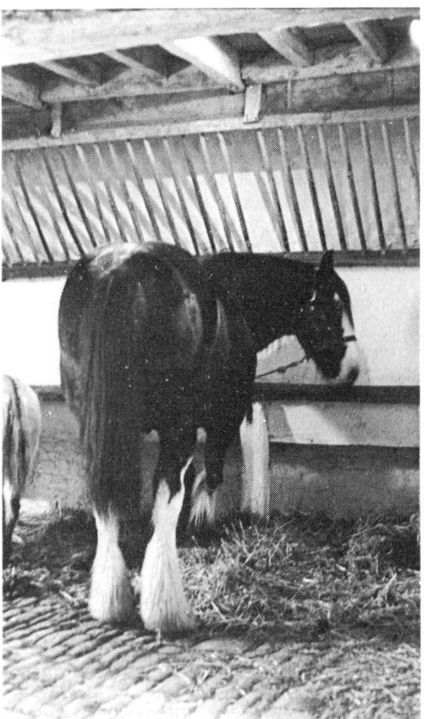

Above: *This stable of mellow Cotswold stone was built as a barn c.1650. The original thatched roof was raised and replaced with stone. It is now part of Cogges Farm Museum, Witney, Oxfordshire.*

Left: *A horse tethered in the old position, parallel to the line of the roof ridge, at Cogges Farm Museum. The rack is filled through a slot in the loft floor.*

hooks for harness, either near each horse or grouped in the harness room. Each stall had a tethering ring, a trough and a rack. Where filling was not done directly from the overhead loft, it was done past the tethered horse. This was in contrast to the custom in cowsheds, which were filled from a separate gangway running past the head end of the stalls. Victorian invention brought numbers of purpose-made materials and fittings. Non-slip fired clay pavings and special drain fittings were added to a growing range of ventilators, ironmongery and other components. Horse care became better and more humane, supported by more durable, lighter and cleaner stables.

*This building next to William Cavendish's Riding House at Bolsover Castle, Derbyshire, is believed to have been stables and was designed by Huntingdon Smythson, c.1640.*

# STABLES WITH HOUSES

## STATELY HOMES AND STATELY STABLES

The stables of stately homes were the most splendid of all. Many had massive entrance arches, spacious yards and great clock-towers, carefully planned and built with costly materials and rich ornament. These lavish stables were integral parts of the architectural compositions of the great houses. They shared in the glory of how the house looked: a classical-style house with classical stables, a Gothic Revival house with Gothic Revival stables, and so on. These stables reflected the position of horse ownership in fashionable country life. Horses were essential for transport and many sporting pursuits, but for most wealthy households horses were also an enthusiasm. Horses were an ideal expression of conspicuous expenditure (a forerunner of cars in more ways than one). Stables were to be seen as well as to be useful; they were to display wealth as well as to shelter horses.

Great-house stables as a building type emerge clearly from the late sixteenth and early seventeenth centuries, when, from the reign of Elizabeth I, a new nobility was building new great houses. Renaissance architectural ideas began to be imported and before long were manifest in new buildings. Appearances were often more vigorous than restful, as the bleakness of the middle ages was left behind.

An early example, now lost, was proposed at Wollaton Hall, Nottinghamshire (*c.*1580). It was formally sited on an axis in a planned landscape. It was probably a long multi-storeyed block with central entrance. Two groups of stalls, running across the block and bisected by the entrance, sheltered twelve horses. Another lost early example was designed by the architect Smythson at Welbeck Abbey, Nottinghamshire (1625). The decorated two-storey exterior had classical central entrance, pedimented windows and small domed pavilions projecting at each end of the block. Fifteen stalls were placed side by side across the interior. About ten years later robust-looking stables were built at Bolsover Castle, Derbyshire, and others in 1656 at Thorpe Hall, Peterborough. Two years earlier, stables for the former

Brenley Manor, near Faversham, Kent, were built. They still survive. Seven stalls fill a handsome near-symmetrical brick block with a loft above. The style of many of the stables of the time resembled that of the houses which they served but was rather less exuberant. Most early interiors have been altered, but there is a seventeenth-century one at Dunster Castle, Somerset, where it looks very massive. At Peover Hall, Cheshire, is a finely ornamented interior of 1654.

## GEORGIAN STABLES

Growing national wealth brought more and bigger great houses – and larger stables. Scale and dignity gradually replaced forcefulness and vigour. Symmetrical Palladian houses were built, with a main central block linked by colonnades to flanking wings. These wings contained stables and other ancillary buildings such as kitchens and chapel. It was considered desirable for the whole house complex to give an impression of large size and the stables contributed to this effect. With larger houses, a single elongated stable block was not enough, so stables were grouped on two or more sides of a court. Occasionally several courts were needed to house horses, carriages, feed and harness. Often staff quarters were on the first floor.

These features were evident in Vanbrugh's original design for Castle Howard, North Yorkshire (1702). The central house block was to be symmetrically flanked by a large stable court on one side and a kitchen court on the other. The design of the cruciform stable court was about 44 metres (144 feet) wide and there were nearly fifty stalls in eight separate and mostly differing rooms. Even this immense composition was to be outdone at Blenheim, Oxfordshire (1705), where Vanbrugh intended a rectangular stable court of about 48 by 41 metres (about 157 by 135 feet) with nearly sixty stalls. This was stable architecture at its most monumental.

Wherever a fine house arose, there were stables. Landowners vied with one another and lively stylistic developments touched the appearance of stables as much as that of houses. Among a wealth of eighteenth-century examples were Seaton Delaval, Northumberland (1768), and Leoni's Latham Hall, Lancashire, with a rectangular stable wing 29 by 15 metres (95 by 48 feet), comprising 28 stalls in five rooms. The stables by the same architect at Moor Park, Hertfordshire (1720), had 38 stalls in six different-sized rooms. One had back-to-back stalls and a central gangway and the others had single rows of stalls. At James Paine's Belford Hall, Northumberland (*c.*1755), the stable wing had twenty stalls in two blocks. The exterior had a classical

*Stables complete the symmetry: block plan of Moor Park, Hertfordshire, a country house of 1720. Stables, left, balance ancillary buildings, right. The main house is in the centre block. Six separate stables, with space for 38 horses, are grouped round a courtyard.*

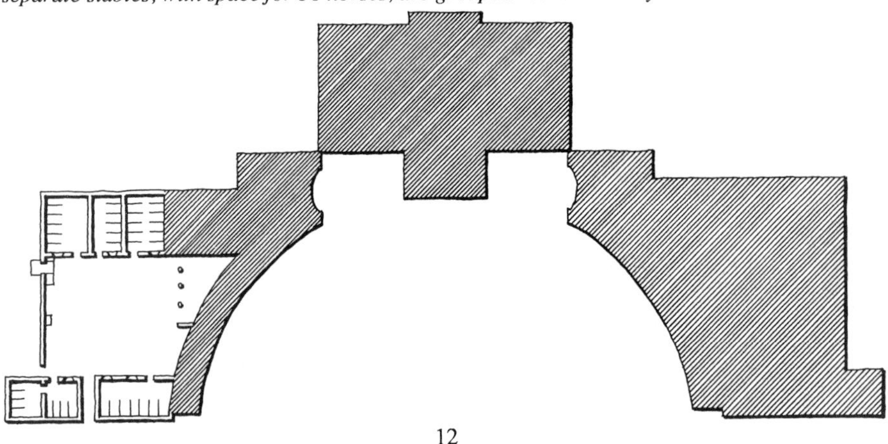

*The stable block at Dunster Castle, Somerset. Within is a range of eight well preserved later seventeenth-century stalls.*

*Symmetrical E-shaped stable range at Audley End, Essex. This brick building with characteristic central lantern is believed to be Jacobean in origin.*

*Stables in the park. A classical stone block fronts two courts at Dyrham Park, Avon, designed by William Talman, 1698. The higher block, left, is part of the main house.*

pediment and carved masonry which blended with the house. Paine also designed a very ornate block at Chatsworth, Derbyshire (1756-63), with eighty stalls, and decorated with blind-arcaded walls, a massive coat of arms, and a clock-tower with cupola. The stable block at Tredegar House, Newport, Gwent (before 1727), stands at a respectful distance from the main house. It contains a central entrance with stables on one side and a riding school on the other. The decorated frontage (brick, like the house) is flanked by

*Gothic Revival: a pointed-head archway, battlements and windows set the style of the stables at Burghley House, Stamford, Lincolnshire, built in the 1760s when 'Capability' Brown improved the estate.*

Above: *An arch, clock and cupola are typical features at the centre of the symmetrical eighteenth-century façade of the stable block at the stately home of Shugborough, Staffordshire.*

Below left: *The battlemented parapet and pointed arches of these stables at Berkeley, Gloucestershire, c.1800, recall the far older castle nearby. The front is brick but the back and sides are of stone, as are the large water troughs.*

Below right: *Triumphal arch entrance to the stables of Goodwood House, West Sussex. A refined classical design with pairs of Doric columns supporting an elegant frieze, designed by Sir William Chambers 1757-63.*

Above: *The massive arch beneath the clock-tower leads to the stable courtyard of the now lost Langton House, Blandford Forum, Dorset. The architect was C. R. Cockerell in 1827.*

Below left: *The view from the churchyard at Avebury, Wiltshire, of former stables with exuberant weather-vane, bell and clock. The building is now a museum.*

Below right: *Interior with loose-boxes, at Breamore House. Note the smart cast iron posts, the non-projecting door handle, the rounded stone door jamb and the impervious floor.*

*Georgian repose at Breamore House, Hampshire. The central entrance bay is decorated with a circular window in the pediment and four stone pilasters below.*

two projecting pavilions.

Plans were varied with long rows of stalls, small groups of stalls, back-to-back groups and varied first-floor accommodation. There was wide scope to follow the needs and fancies of owners and designers. An example of the unusual was William Porden's stables at the Royal Pavilion, Brighton, (1804). About sixty stalls were arranged, some in opposed long blocks and others radially, under a 24 metre (80 foot) dome. The Indian revival style was to influence Nash's nearby Pavilion. The extravagant cost was nearly £80,000.

Medium-sized country houses also flourished in the eighteenth century. Again, stables often shared the wall and roof materials of the house and at least some of the ornamentation. Countless examples existed at all the middle-ranking and smaller houses. Some were by recognised architects but others were anonymous and more like the better farm stables. If a loose distinction can be made, it is between the formal, 'polite' quality of domestic stables and the more utilitarian and vernacular nature of farm stables.

The London homes of the aristocracy needed stables just as did the country houses. Perhaps the grandest was William Kent's Royal Mews (1732) on the site of the present National Gallery. A magnificent block, 72 metres (235 feet) long, with arched façade and attic storey housed 56 horses. More modest was Robert Adam's design for Lord Derby's house (1773) in Grosvenor Square. The stables were not big enough for much architectural display, which was confined to the house. The stables were packed closely at the rear of the deep narrow plot and were reached from a back street. The eleven stalls were arranged in two rows back-to-back, one row of eight narrow stalls and the other of three wider ones. The intervening gangway was partitioned along its length. This showed that even where space was tight, some horses were to be segregated and better housed than others. Above the stables were two hay lofts, and adjoining were two coach-houses with groom's room above.

*Mid eighteenth century stables at Woburn Abbey, Bedfordshire. The architect, Henry Flitcroft, has used pairs of columns to emphasise the entrance in a carefully controlled composition.*

## VICTORIAN AND EDWARDIAN STABLES

The Victorians continued vigorous country-house, and hence stable, building. Standards and fashions were set at the top which filtered down to new medium-sized houses and then to smaller ones. A succession of architectural styles came and went as classicism gave way to revivals of pointed-arch Gothic, Elizabethan and others. Reposeful Georgian symmetry gave way to assertive asymmetry, with romantic silhouette of gables, turrets and chimneys. House planning became more complicated with the Victorian love of classification and hierarchy. Each activity about the house had to have its own separate space. This could mean separate stables for carriage horses, riding horses, hunters, strangers' horses and post horses. In the running of country houses, often needing dozens of servants, the stables occupied a vital and warmly regarded role.

Published guidance about stables became far more plentiful. Leading concerns were draught-free ventilation and damp-free floors. One authority, J. C. Loudon, advocated large, cool, well ventilated, south-east facing stables. Typical recommendations were large windows, 3.3 metres (11 feet) ceiling height and high-level ventilation through tubes passing up through the roof. Flat hard-brick floors with various types of drainage were preferred to rearward sloping stone floors. Removable slatted timber floors were proposed, but not much used. Opinion was divided over the merits of iron and wooden hay racks. Stall partition heel-posts were not to be too tall, to avoid head injuries. Increasingly loose-boxes were preferred to stalls.

Growing concern for horses' health, affected by ventilation, damp and space, echoed human affairs, where there was anxiety about the fast-growing towns. What was bad for slum-dwellers was seen also as bad for horses and could be remedied in similar ways. Robert Kerr had a typically practical view of stable design aims in 1865: '...so to lodge [the horse] that his food shall be readily supplied, his stall easily cleaned and well drained, and the air kept, if not absolutely fresh, at least sufficiently so...' Kerr dismissed stables with central gangway and stalls each side because of poor light and air. He approved of tile-faced walls, non-absorbent ceilings, southerly aspect and high-level ventilators. Harness and saddle rooms were to be dry and fitted with hooks, brackets, glass case, hanging for whips and lamps, a press for rugs and horsecloths, and drawers for brushes. An open-fronted

Above left: *A cast iron window frame, a mid nineteenth-century (or earlier) detail, at Frenchay Park, Avon.*

Above right: *Windows of many shapes adorn the delightful central bay of the Gothic Revival style stable wing at Ashton Court, Bristol. The turrets contain stairs linking the ground-floor stables with the first-floor staff quarters.*

Below left: *The heavy stone design of this massive clock-tower of 1864 at Arlington Court, Devon, reflects mid-Victorian confidence. It is now used as a carriage museum by the National Trust.*

Below right: *The stylish interior at Ashton Court. The loose-box on the right has Gothic Revival style cast iron posts, complete with miniature pinnacles and cusps. It is today used by the horses for the Lord Mayor of Bristol's processional coach.*

grooming shed could act as a vestibule to the stable. A horse bath needed 'a capacious cistern overhead, with the usual shower-bath apparatus'. The suggested stable-yard size was 12 by 15-30 metres (40 by 50-100 feet). Large stables could have a covered ride round the yard for exercising sick horses and use in bad weather. Water supply, drainage and dung-pit position were all considered. A clock-tower was thought essential.

The importance of large stables is obvious from Kerr's cost estimate (at the time small terraced houses cost about £100):

| | £ |
|---|---|
| Carriage stables, 8 stalls | 280 |
| Nag stables, 6 stalls | 210 |
| Hunter stables, 6 stalls | 240 |
| Strangers' stables, 4 stalls | 160 |
| Loose-boxes, 4 | 200 |
| Carriage house, 6 bays | 240 |
| Harness room, 8 horses | 80 |
| Saddle room, 12 horses | 120 |
| Harness cleaning room | 30 |
| Grooming shed | 80 |
| Horse bath and porch | 80 |
| Open carriage shed, 2 bays | 60 |
| Stable yard | 300 |
| Dung yard | 50 |
| Boiler house | 50 |
| Smithy and shoeing shed | 50 |
| Clock turret and clock | 250 |
| 6 hay lofts etc | 360 |
| 10 servants' rooms | 400 |
| Mess room, staircases & wcs | 220 |
| | — |
| | £3460 |

This was a bargain compared with £5000 for a 22 horse stable at Lyme Hall, Cheshire (1864). This was a luxury job, with eighteen loose-boxes and smart buff-coloured glazed interior wall tiles with chocolate-coloured bands. Stables at Grey Towers, near Middlesbrough (1873), for the same amount housed about twenty horses and had an unusual glass-roofed yard. The size of the 118 horse Royal Stables, Windsor (1842), must have been almost unsurpassed and, at £70,000, so must the cost. Among architecturally notable examples were Pugin's splendid pinnacled and battlemented design at Scarisbrick Hall, near Southport, Merseyside (1837-45), and Teulon's equally spirited Shadwell Park, Thetford, Norfolk (1856-60).

Striking exteriors were matched by carefully thought-out interiors. Pennethorne's brick design at Marlborough House, London (1863), with 45 stalls and twelve loose-boxes, was excellently equipped. There

*Early Victorian severity in a stable block of c.1845 which once belonged to Uffington House, Lincolnshire. The rooftop box-louvre vents suggest practical concerns.*

Left: *French Renaissance style for the stable block of Rendcomb House, Gloucestershire.*

Right: *The stable courtyard by Burges at Cardiff Castle shows his use of dramatic silhouette and stout timber-framing.*

were coloured iron fittings, vitreous enamelled corn bins, 'friction guard rollers' to prevent biting of corn bins, racks and tanks, and devices to avoid horses' heads becoming trapped in hay racks. Skirtings were bluish-grey marble and the slate water reservoirs had hinged seats for the men. Among this wealth no dangerous small projections were to be found. Equal attention to detail was seen in some smaller stables, where there might be iron drainage channels, bevelled-edge Staffordshire blue floor bricks, and gas laid on. Victorian invention was also found at the four-horse Hersham Lodge stables, Walton-on-Thames, Surrey (1868). Here there were experimental concrete walls, patent revolving door shutters and combined roof ventilators and lantern lights with plate-glass louvres.

The 1870s were a turning point after which major house building declined and display in stables was moderated. At the same time accommodation and care for horses continued gradually to improve. More space was given to each horse, with preference for the more costly and bigger loose-boxes of, say, 3.6 by 3.0 metres (12 by 10 feet) over stalls. There were more 'hospital boxes', usually sited to avoid cross-infection. Another sign of rising standards (though exceptional) was central heating, at Avery Hill, Greenwich (1885-91). Special fittings included drawbars which extended from stall partitions to block gangways and stop horses which had broken loose. There were also hollow iron heel-posts connected to underground ducts to give ventilation from the tops of the posts. By 1900, if not before, most new mangers were iron rather than wood.

A typical example of late Victorian practice was at Otford, near Sevenoaks, Kent (1890). Brick and tile buildings were informally grouped around three sides of a yard, in contrast to earlier rigid layouts. Seven loose-boxes were provided, each with direct access to the yard (not along a gangway). There were also four stalls, a coach-house, harness room, coachman's living rooms and lofts. An example of a smaller establishment was built at Didsbury, Manchester (1888). An L-shaped block contained two loose-boxes, a stall, washing bay and sick box in one wing. In the other were a coach-house and heated harness room. On the first floor of the brick and tiled block were a loft and living space. There were ornamental gables and a turret which gave ventilation and space for a corn bin and

*Plan of a late design for a stable courtyard at Childwick Bury, St Albans, Hertfordshire, c.1900. Key: B, loose-box; C, coach-house; CW, carriage wash; F, fodder; H, harness; HC, harness cleaning; K, kitchen; MH, mash house; MS, mess room; S, stall; T, tack. Dark shading denotes two storeys (loft and staff quarters). The arrow shows the archway entrance.*

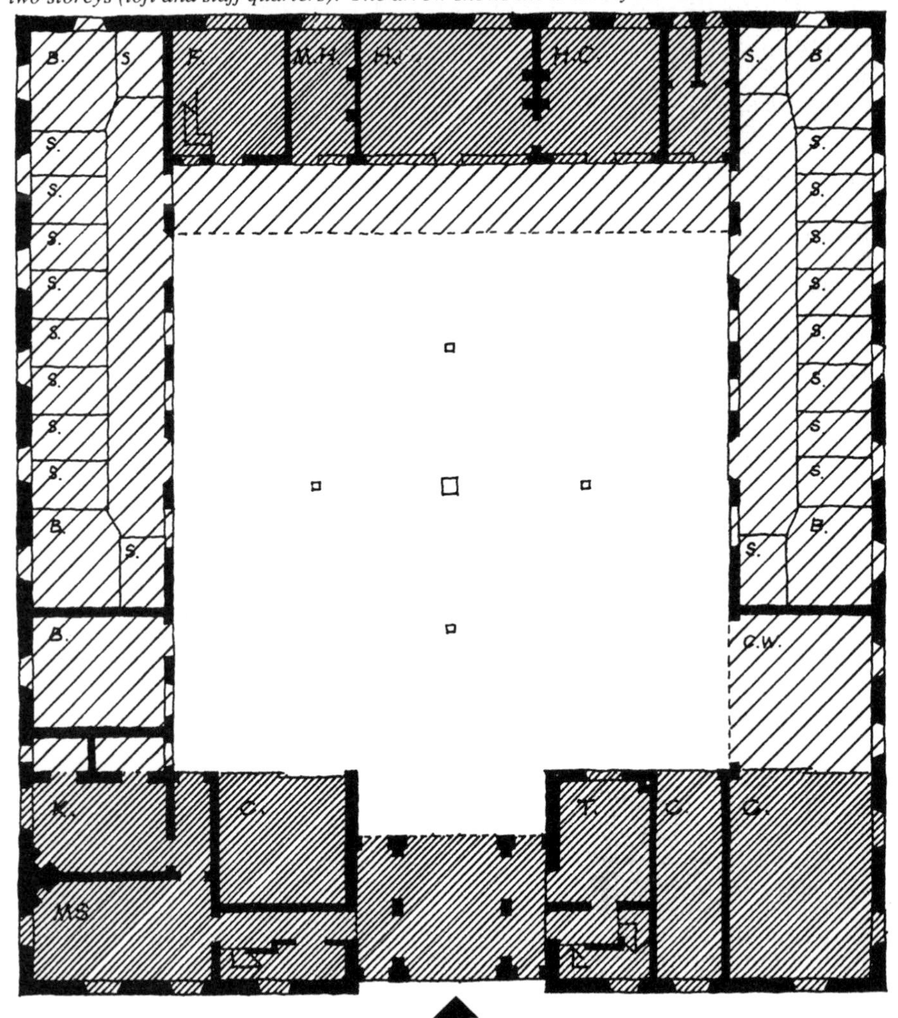

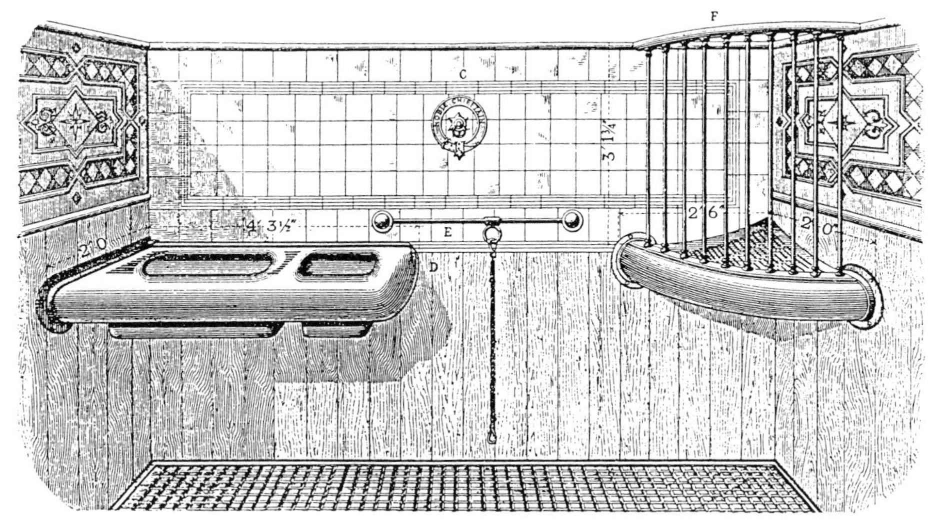


*Stable fittings, illustrated in the Milton trade catalogue: manger and hay-rack sets, suitable for a stall or loose-box.*

shute, all topped with a cupola and weather-vane.

Compact urban stables at the rear of large terraced town houses continued to be built through the nineteenth century. In Brunswick Square, Brighton (*c.*1830), for example, there were simple four-stall stables behind each imposing six-floor house. Similar mews stables became common in districts such as Belgravia. A development

*Stable fittings: brackets, hooks and other small fittings from the Milton catalogue.*

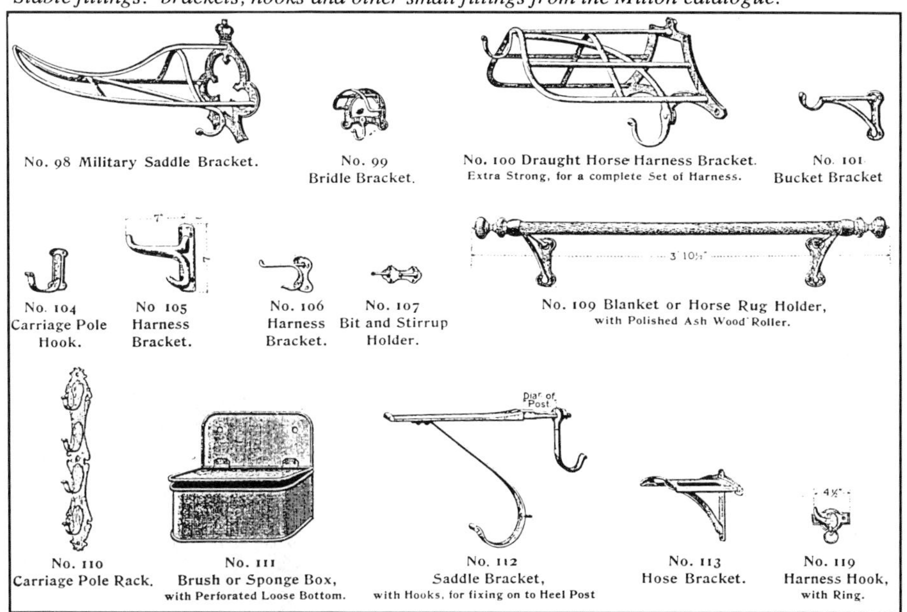

Above: *A London mews entrance: Hyde Park Gardens Mews, London W2. A screen wall and arch were not provided in all cases.*

Left: *Stable fittings: Milton loose-box doors with iron posts and timber boarding. Compare with the interiors at Breamore House and Ashton Court, pages 16 and 19.*

*A late nineteenth-century stable in the suburbs, at Penarth, South Glamorgan. Stone piers stand beside the gateway to the stable yard, with the house off right. The stable door is in the centre, below the loft door. The coach-house door is on the right.*

for the Marquis of Westminster (*c*.1865) had mews stables built over basements. Each house had three stalls and a loose-box, as well as two carriage spaces and a harness recess. Above the stables were a loft and coachman's flat. Some superior developments were embellished by a lofty arch in a screen wall at the mews entrance, but seldom much more. In smaller developments the mews could be mean in size and materials. Some first floors, as in Pimlico, were reached by space-saving external ladders. At worst, loft living was unhealthy – and problems could spread. In the cholera-stricken 1850s it was complained that 'the mansions of the upper classes, so near to the mews, are well supplied with stable smells... The effect, on delicate ladies especially... is most injurious.'

The urban tradition of compact functional stables and the rural tradition of spacious monumental ones overlapped in the wealthier suburbs. Every villa of any pretension had a small stable and carriage-house – a sure sign of substance and independence. The stable was likely to be compact through necessity, and lightly embellished if possible. Many such stables had only a short working life. Before the First World War horseless carriages were cutting the need for stables. While country horses kept for pleasure were probably enjoying their highest standard of living so far, horses for workaday transport were passing away.

*Later inn stables at West Tanfield, North Yorkshire. Fine painted lettering, the weather-vane and 'kneelers' on the stone gable impart a sense of distinction, though some openings have been changed.*

# STABLES FOR BUSINESSES AND MODERN STABLES

Most stables for businesses and institutions were more functional than decorative. Many also were on a large or very large scale. The most romantic enterprise (at least in hindsight) of this type was stage-coaching. There were stables for horses working cumbersome coach services on a few key routes out of London in the seventeenth century. Before that, stables were to be found in the yards of medieval inns, as at the timber-framed George Inn at Dorchester-on-Thames, Oxfordshire (*c.*1500). By the mid eighteenth century better services on new turnpike roads required new coaching inns and stables at every 12-15 mile (19-24 km) stage. By the end of the eighteenth century there was at least one inn with stables in every market town. The heyday of coaching came in the 1820s and 1830s when an estimated 150,000 horses were used. At Hounslow, the busy first westbound stage out of London, as many as 2500 were said to be stabled. London coaching inns acted as national passenger termini. The Belle Sauvage on Ludgate Hill had four hundred horses and the Spread Eagle, Gracechurch Street, had as many as 1800.

A typical coaching inn had an urbane Georgian façade and a generous storey-high opening in the front giving access to a paved yard surrounded by stables and outbuildings. The scene has been celebrated as a romantic backdrop on countless Christmas cards. Examples of coaching inns survive widely in high streets such as that at Amersham, Buckinghamshire. Traces of their stables are fragmentary but can still be found.

The collapse of stage-coaching brought about by the railways was far from the end of stables for public transport. The decline of coaching horses was more than balanced by the increase of cab and other horses. Inns and hotels continued to need stabling for travellers' horses, even if the appeal of old coaching days was lessened. Horse-drawn omnibus services in London were begun in 1829 and the London General Omnibus Company had about eight hundred horse omnibuses in 1855. The same firm twenty years later built large stables at Bromley, Bow, for the sizable sum of £3600, and at Goldhawk Road, Shepherds Bush, for £2300. Every large town had its counterpart. At Newcastle upon Tyne in 1880 the tramway company built Percy Street depot with stalls for nearly two hundred horses. These stables could be converted to steam-engine sheds if needed. Most public transport stables of this sort were basic, if not mean. Many stall divisions were only a plank suspended horizontally edgeways from two chains from the ceiling. *The Builder* noted: '...economy of space and construction is sure to be made such a prominent considera-tion... The rough ways of an omnibus company's stables, where...the harness is hung up alongside the horse, are no school for

Below: *Early inn stables at the George Inn, Dorchester-on-Thames, Oxfordshire. View of the stable yard seen through the covered way leading from the street. Stables occupied the right-hand end of the timber-framed and timber-clad range of c.1500.*

Above: *The Red Lion at Salisbury, Wiltshire, a former coaching inn. The high arch opening off the street betrays the original function. The façade was built in 1820, but fourteenth-century work survives in the courtyard.*

private stable building.'

Lying between the quality extremes of crude omnibus stables and sumptuous country-house stables were livery stables. Here Victorian citizens could pay to house their carriages and have them horsed and attended. This gave the convenience and prestige of carriage ownership with less expense and care. Some livery stables were sizable businesses. One built at Sefton Park, Liverpool, in 1884 had 44 stalls and twelve loose-boxes. Because of the tightness of the site some carriages were stored on the first floor and lifted by hoist.

Inland waterways were well supplied with stables both in their pre-railway heyday and during the long decline which followed. Some canal stables were quite big, as at Sheepcote Street, Birmingham, where there is a horseshoe-shaped block of 1840 for 49 horses, round a central courtyard. One access is from the street and the other is up a ramp into the courtyard from the lower-

Above: *The canal stable at Sheepcote Street, Birmingham, seen from the canal. The horseshoe-shaped block is visible below the tallest crane. The towpath is one storey lower than street level. A ramp in the stable yard links the towpath and street levels.*

Left: *The same canal stable seen from the street. The horseshoe-shaped yard lies beyond the wooden gates between the two lodges.*

level towpath. Elsewhere on the canals there was a great variety of stables. Some were in free-standing waterside blocks, as at Llanymynech, Powys, on the Shropshire Union Canal. Some were part of lengthsmen's cottages, as in the unusual cylindrical 1790s examples on the Thames and Severn Canal. There the stable was the lowest of three vertically stacked circular rooms. Others, generally more plain, were attached to canal pubs, as at the Navigation Inn near Braunston, Northamptonshire, on the Oxford Canal.

Railways, villains of stage-coach and canal history, also owned surprising numbers of stables. Most housed horses for short-distance haulage between railhead and customer. The Great Western Railway alone owned twenty thousand horses in 1914. Typical GWR stables were carefully detailed single-storey buildings of strident red and dark blue brick and slate. Appropriately for a confident company at the height of the Empire, the buildings look to have been built to last for ever. One at Park Royal, near Ealing, had a line of twelve stalls and a forage store. There was ample ventilation through window vents, high and low level wall vents and built-up timber roof-ridge vents. Expressing care (if not always elegance) in their design were the safe rounded (or bull-nose) bricks on all wall angles and window sills. Drainage channels were ingeniously made of reused rails laid on their sides.

What industrial stables lacked in quality they made up for in variety. Some well-off firms could afford good standards, but countless less prosperous ones did not manage so well. At one extreme were rough and ready sheds and underground stabling in the mines (there were 17,000 horses underground in South Wales alone in 1913). At the other extreme were urban multi-storey stable blocks, some mixed with warehousing or other uses.

Above: *Looking out of the entrance to the stable block at Dowlais ironworks, Mid Glamorgan. Metal 'spiders' help prevent the rubble wall from bulging. In the distance beyond the elliptical arch is barren hillside.*

Below: *Warehouse stables: a diagrammatic first-floor plan of a five-storey block built in Charles Street, Drury Lane, London, 1884. The horse on the extreme right will follow the kerb line to the front entrance (not visible), cross through ground-floor warehousing and climb the ramp, mid-left. On the first floor are twelve stalls, four loose-boxes and a harness room. Staff quarters are in the row of rooms running from the top corner to the right-hand corner. Three floors above contain more warehousing and staff quarters.*

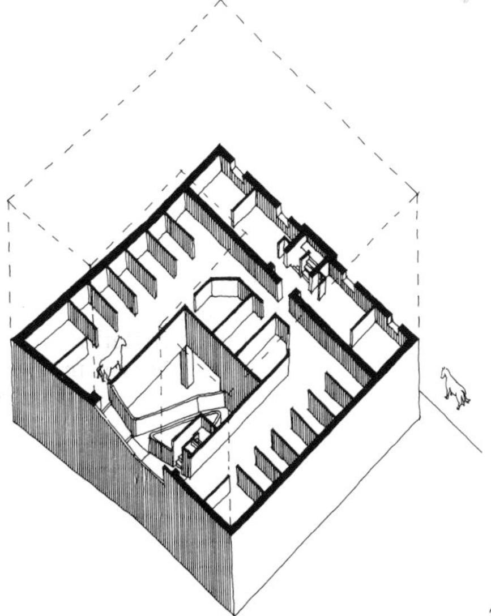

An example of these specialised mixed-use buildings was built at Charles Street, Drury Lane, London, in 1884. It had stores on the ground floor, and twelve stalls and three loose-boxes on the first floor, reached by an unroofed ramp. The three floors above this held warehousing and flats for employees. Another example was the Co-operative Society stables in Battenberg Road, Leicester. This was a three-storey block with ground-floor cartsheds, first-floor stables reached by ramp, and second-floor loft. A further variation was the two-storey Crosse and Blackwell building of 1876 in Crown Street, Soho, London. It had space for four horses, eighteen vans and fodder store on the ground floor, and 35 stalls, one loose-box, more fodder and a stableman's flat on the first floor. There were also stables without number for breweries, brickyards, dairies, merchants, retailers and others. There were stables for heavy dray horses and stables for delivery-van ponies; all found a place in the midst of the compact Victorian town. An oddity was the costermongers' donkey stables built adjoining the Columbia Market, Bethnal Green, in 1877. It housed nearly fifty donkeys and ponies and was made of corrugated iron sheeting with timber partitions.

An uncharted variety of stables remains. There were cavalry barracks stables, police stables and smart (though often inaccessible) racing stables. A well appointed example built in 1864 for the Newmarket Hotels Company provided one hundred loose-boxes and stalls at a cost of £10,000. Another specialised stable type was built for fire stations, where speed was vital. The stables were placed as close as possible to the waiting fire engines. Harness was suspended over the horses, ready to be lowered at a moment's notice. Aldershot fire station (1907) even had electrically opening stable doors. A limit to specialisation is perhaps reached with the now lost stabling for the thirty military horses shipped to the Crimea in 1855 aboard Brunel's SS *Great Britain*.

Most stables built since the First World War represented a triumph of utility over appearance. Low building costs and efficiency in day-to-day running overshadowed visual display. Most new stables were for horses kept for leisure and pleasure. Private owners built small stables in paddocks and near farm buildings. Also there were stables for riding schools and trekking centres.

These, the latest generation of stables, were laid out to save costly labour. Among newer features were utility boxes for grooming, shoeing and washing, and loose-boxes entirely replacing stalls. Walls were of concrete blocks or timber-framed and timber-clad. Roof pitches were lower, often with wide front overhang to give shelter. There were concrete pavings, sliding doors, electric lighting and better fire and security precautions. Appearances were lighter and more plain than before, faintly echoing the functionalism of the architectural modern movement. The idea that stables were special and worthy of decoration had faded along with old distinctions between stables of different type of owner. Lost character was a price paid for keeping most horses in healthier quarters than ever before. Priori-

Left: *A close-up of a row of quayside stables at Porlock Weir, Somerset, some of which have been converted to new uses. Note the roof glazing and ridge box-louvre vents. Inside are four loose-boxes.*

Right: *A fine row of former stables converted to shops, off High Street, Marlborough, Wiltshire.*

*Modern stables, plain but efficient, at Middleham, North Yorkshire. They are built of concrete blocks with a corrugated sheet roof, like the adjoining farm buildings.*

ties had moved decisively from bricks and mortar to the animals they sheltered and the people who tended them; who is to say this was a backward step?

Twentieth-century losses of stables have been very great: working horses have become few; small dispersed horse ownership has replaced large and centralised ownership; and old stables have decayed and sometimes obstructed new land uses. Losses were greatest in the towns and among business users. But this sad state is far from the whole story. First came a revival in the appreciation of horses. Now there is growing interest in historic buildings and conservation. Stables for horses must be the first aim, but where old stables are no longer needed they can be imaginatively reused. Bowood, Wiltshire, showed a way in 1955 with 'the grandest stables conversion in England'. And in other places old stables have found new uses as art centres and galleries, workshops, playrooms, pubs and shops.

# FURTHER READING

Published information about stables, at the time of writing, is scattered widely and in small parts. Guide books to many stately homes and some other historic buildings contain a few relevant sentences or a paragraph. Some studies of important architects or periods (for example, Girouard, below) also may be helpful. Farm stables are better covered.


Brunskill, R. W. *Traditional Farm Buildings of Britain*. Gollancz, 1988.

Girouard, M. *Victorian Country Houses*. Yale University Press, 1985.

Peters, J. E. C. *Discovering Traditional Farm Buildings*. Shire, 1981.

Pevsner, N., *et al*. *Buildings of England* and *Buildings of Wales* series. Penguin, various dates.

Smith, Peter C. *Design and Construction of Stables and Ancillary Buildings*. J. A. Allen, 1967.

Wiliam, E. *Historical Farm Buildings of Wales*. John Donald, Edinburgh, 1986.

# PLACES TO VISIT

Nearly all major houses offer something to see (although not all stables are open to the public or used for their original purpose). The examples here are a beginning; the possibilities are almost endless. Farm stables are less accessible, but some worthwhile examples are listed below.

*Acton Scott Working Farm Museum*, Wenlock Lodge, Acton Scott, Church Stretton, Shropshire SY6 6QN. Telephone: 06946 306 or 307.

*Arlington Court*, Arlington, Barnstaple, Devon EX31 4LP. Telephone: 0271 850296. National Trust. Stables in use; they also contain a museum of carriages.

*Avoncroft Museum of Buildings*, Redditch Road, Stoke Heath, Bromsgrove, Worcestershire B60 4JR. Telephone: 0527 31363 or 31886.

*Bass Museum, Visitor Centre and Shire Horse Stables,* Horninglow Street, Burton on Trent, Staffordshire DE14 1JZ. Telephone: 0283 511000.

*Breamore House*, Breamore, Fordingbridge, Hampshire SP6 2DF. Telephone: 0725 22468 or 22233 or 22270. Contains a carriage museum.

*Cogges Farm Museum*, Church Lane, Cogges, Witney, Oxfordshire OX8 6LA. Telephone: 0993 772602.

*Dunster Castle*, Dunster, Minehead, Somerset TA24 6SL. Telephone: 064382 314. National Trust.

*Shugborough Park Farm* (Staffordshire County Museum), Shugborough, Milford, Stafford ST17 0XB. Telephone: 0889 881388.

*Tyrwhitt-Drake Museum of Carriages*, Archbishop's Stables, Mill Street, Maidstone, Kent ME15 6YE. Telephone: 0622 754497.

*Weald and Downland Open Air Museum*, Singleton, Chichester, West Sussex PO18 0EU. Telephone: 024363 348.

*Welsh Folk Museum*, St Fagans, Cardiff, South Glamorgan CF5 6XB. Telephone: 0222 569441.

*Whitbread Hop Farm,* Beltring, Paddock Wood, Tonbridge TN12 6PY. Telephone: 0622 872068.

*Imposing early stable block at Arbury Hall, Warwickshire. This classically influenced design with three ornate gables is believed to date from about the middle of the seventeenth century.*